"9Marks, as a ministry, has taken basic biblical teaching about the church and put it into the hands of pastors. Bobby, by way of these study guides, has taken this teaching and delivered it to the person in the pew. I am unaware of any other tool that so thoroughly and practically helps Christians understand God's plan for the local church. I can't wait to use these studies in my own congregation."

> **Jeramie Rinne,** Senior Pastor, South Shore Baptist Church, Hingham, Massachusetts

"Bobby Jamieson has done local church pastors an incredible service by writing these study guides. Clear, biblical, and practical, they introduce the biblical basis for a healthy church. But more importantly, they challenge and equip church members to be part of the process of improving their own church's health. The studies work for individual, small group, and larger group settings. I have used them for the last year at my own church and appreciate how easy they are to adapt to my own setting. I don't know of anything else like them. Highly recommended!"

> **Michael Lawrence,** Senior Pastor, Hinson Baptist Church, *Biblical Theology in the Life of the Church*

"This is a Bible study that is actually rooted in the Bible and involves actual study. In the 9Marks Healthy Church Study Guides series a new standard has been set for personal theological discovery and corresponding personal application. Rich exposition, compelling questions, and clear syntheses combine to give a guided tour of ecclesiology—the theology of the church. I know of no better curriculum for generating understanding of and involvement in the church than this. It will be a welcome resource in our church for years to come."

> **Rick Holland,** Senior Pastor, Mission Road Bible Church, Prairie Village, Kansas

"In America today we have the largest churches in the history of our nation, but the least amount of impact for Christ's kingdom. Slick marketing and finely polished vision statements are a foundation of sand. The 9Marks Healthy Church Study Guides series is a refreshing departure from church-growth materials, towards an in-depth study of God's Word that will equip God's people with his vision for his Church. These study guides will lead local congregations to abandon secular methodologies for church growth and instead rely on Christ's principles for developing healthy, God-honoring assemblies."

> **Carl J. Broggi,** Senior Pastor, Community Bible Church, Beaufort, South Carolina; President, Search the Scriptures Radio Ministry

"Anyone who loves Jesus will love what Jesus loves. The Bible clearly teaches that Jesus loves the church. He knows about and cares for individual churches and wants them to be spiritually healthy and vibrant. Not only has Jesus laid down his life for the church but he has also given many instructions in his Word regarding how churches are to live and function in the world. This series of Bible studies by 9Marks shows how Scripture teaches these things. Any Christian who works through this curriculum, preferably with other believers, will be helped to see in fresh ways the wisdom, love, and power of God in establishing the church on earth. These studies are biblical, practical, and accessible. I highly recommend this curriculum as a useful tool that will help any church embrace its calling to display the glory of God to a watching world."

> **Thomas Ascol,** Senior Pastor, Grace Baptist Church of Cape Coral, Florida; Executive Director, Founders Ministries

9MARKS HEALTHY CHURCH STUDY GUIDES

Built upon the Rock: The Church

Hearing God's Word: Expositional Preaching

The Whole Truth about God: Biblical Theology

God's Good News: The Gospel

Real Change: Conversion

Reaching the Lost: Evangelism

Committing to One Another: Church Membership

Guarding One Another: Church Discipline

Growing One Another: Discipleship in the Church

Leading One Another: Church Leadership

REACHING
THE LOST:
EVANGELISM

Bobby Jamieson
Mark Dever, General Editor
Jonathan Leeman, Managing Editor

HEALTHY CHURCH STUDY GUIDES

:: CROSSWAY

WHEATON, ILLINOIS

CONTENTS

INTRODUCTION

What does the local church mean to you?

Maybe you love your church. You love the people. You love the preaching, the singing. You can't wait to show up on Sunday, and you cherish fellowship with other church members throughout the week.

Maybe the church is just a place you show up to a couple times a month. You sneak in late, duck out early.

We at 9Marks are convinced that the local church is God's plan for displaying his glory to the nations. And we want to help you catch and live out that vision, together with your whole church.

The 9Marks Healthy Church Study Guides are a series of six- or seven-week studies on each of the "nine marks of a healthy church" plus one introductory study. These nine marks are the core convictions of our ministry. To provide a quick introduction to them, we've included a chapter from Mark Dever's book *What Is a Healthy Church?* with each study. We don't claim that these nine marks are the most important things about the church or the only important things about the church. But we do believe that they are biblical and therefore are helpful for churches.

So, in these studies, we're going to work through the biblical foundations and practical applications of each one. The ten studies are:

- *Built upon the Rock: The Church* (the introductory study)
- *Hearing God's Word: Expositional Preaching*
- *The Whole Truth about God: Biblical Theology*
- *God's Good News: The Gospel*
- *Real Change: Conversion*
- *Reaching the Lost: Evangelism*
- *Committing to One Another: Church Membership*

- *Guarding One Another: Church Discipline*
- *Growing One Another: Discipleship in the Church*
- *Leading One Another: Church Leadership*

Each session of these studies takes a close look at one or more passages of Scripture and considers how it applies to the life of the whole church. So, we hope that these studies are equally appropriate for Sunday school, small groups, and other contexts where a group of anywhere from two to two-hundred people can come together and discuss God's Word.

These studies are mainly driven by observation, interpretation, and application questions, so get ready to speak up! We also hope that these studies provide opportunities for people to reflect together on their experiences in the church, whatever those experiences may be.

Do you know any really good evangelists? I do. And I'm certainly not one of them.

Some people seem to be able to turn any conversation to Jesus. It doesn't matter if the conversation is about food, the weather, taxes, football, or anything else under the sun—they can get from zero to the gospel in about 5.9 seconds. Yet is it only those people who are called to evangelize? The first session in this study looks at the question, who should evangelize? The answer? Every Christian.

Yet too often our responsibility to evangelize inspires fear rather than excitement, guilt rather than joy. So in order to make sure we're evangelizing for the right reasons, the second session asks, why should we evangelize?

Another reason evangelism can seem intimidating is that we don't really know how to do it. Sessions three through five explore the question, how should we evangelize?

Finally, one great encouragement to our evangelism is that Jesus's evangelism plan is a whole lot bigger than you or me. In fact, it's as big as our local churches. According to Scripture, local churches have a powerful role to play in evangelism, not only by proclaiming the gospel, but also by displaying the gospel in our life together.

The gospel is the best news in the world. Let's jump in and think about how to share it with others.

AN IMPORTANT MARK OF A HEALTHY CHURCH: A BIBLICAL UNDERSTANDING OF EVANGELISM

BY MARK DEVER

(Adapted from chapter 9 of What Is a Healthy Church?*)*

In other volumes in this series, we have described healthy churches as marked by expositional preaching, biblical theology, and a biblical understanding of the gospel and conversion. That means when churches don't teach the Bible and sound doctrine they become unhealthy.

What does an unhealthy church look like? It's a church where the sermons often veer into cliché and repetition. Worse yet, they become moralistic and me-centered, and the gospel is recast as little more than spiritual "self-help." Conversion is viewed as an act of human resolve. And by varying degrees, from bad to worse, the culture of the church is indistinguishable from the secular culture surrounding it.

Such congregations do not herald the tremendous news of salvation in Jesus Christ, to say the least.

EVANGELISM SHAPED BY UNDERSTANDING OF CONVERSION

As we turn in this volume to consider another important mark of a healthy church—a biblical understanding of evangelism—it's worth considering how much our view of this mark will be shaped by our understanding of the previous ones, especially conversion.

On the one hand, if our minds have been shaped by what the Bible teaches about God and how he works, as well as by what it teaches about the gospel and what sinful human beings ultimately need, then a right understanding of evangelism will generally follow. We will attempt to spur on evangelism principally through teaching and meditating on the gospel itself, not through learning methods for sharing it.

I am always heartened by how new Christians seem innately aware of the gracious nature of their salvation. You may even have heard testimonies in the last few months that confess that conversion is the work of God (Eph. 2:8–9). "I was totally lost in sin, but God. . . ."

On the other hand, if what the Bible says about God's work in conversion is left to the side in our churches, then evangelism becomes our doing whatever we can to produce a verbal confession. One sign that a church may not have a biblical understanding of conversion and evangelism is that its membership is markedly larger than its attendance. Such a church should stop and ask why its evangelism produces such a large number of members it never sees yet who feel secure in their salvation. What did we tell them that discipleship in Christ means? What did we teach them about God, sin, and the world?

For all members of the church, but particularly for leaders who have the responsibility of teaching, a biblical understanding of evangelism is crucial.

WHAT IS EVANGELISM?

According to the Bible, Christians are called to care, to plead, and even to persuade unbelievers (2 Cor. 5:11). Yet we are to do so by "setting forth the truth plainly," which means renouncing "secret and shameful ways" (2 Cor. 4:2 NIV).

Evangelism, in other words, is not about doing everything we can to get a person to make a decision for Jesus, much less about imposing our views. Attempting to force a spiritual birth will prove to be as effective as Ezekiel trying to stitch dead, dry bones together to make a person (Ezekiel 37) or as likely as Nicodemus giving himself a new birth in the Spirit (John 3).

Furthermore, evangelism is not the same thing as sharing a personal testimony. It's not the same thing as presenting a rational defense of the faith. It's not even doing works of charity, though all three of these things may accompany evangelism. Nor should evangelism be confused with the results of evangelism, as if to say we've only successfully evangelized when a conversion follows.

No, evangelism is speaking words. It's sharing news. It's being faithful to God by presenting the good news that we discussed in chapter 8—that Christ, by his death and resurrection, has secured a way for a holy God and sinful people to be reconciled. God will produce true conversions when we present this good news (see John 1:13; Acts 18:9–10). In short, evangelism is presenting the good news freely and trusting God to convert people (see Acts 16:14). "Salvation comes from the LORD" (Jonah 2:9 NIV; cf. John 1:12–13).

HOW TO EVANGELIZE

When I evangelize, I attempt to convey three things to people about the decision that must be made about the gospel:

- The decision is costly, so it must be carefully considered (see Luke 9:62).
- The decision is urgent, so make it soon (see Luke 12:20).
- The decision is worth it, so you want to make it (see John 10:10).

This is the message we need to communicate personally to family and friends. This is the message we need to communicate corporately as a whole church.

There are some excellent resources in print about evangelism. For considering the close connection between our understanding of the gospel and the evangelistic methods we use, I recommend Will Metzger's *Tell the Truth* (InterVarsity, 2002), Iain Murray's *The Invitation System* (1991), and *Revival and Revivalism* (Banner of Truth, 1994) , as well as my own *The Gospel and Personal*

Evangelism (Crossway, 2007) and Mack Stiles's *Marks of the Messenger* (InterVarsity, 2010).

Another important mark of a healthy church, then, is a biblical understanding and practice of evangelism. The only true growth is the growth that comes from God and through his people.

WEEK 1
WHO SHOULD EVANGELIZE?

GETTING STARTED

1. *What drew you to this study on evangelism?*

2. *What are you hoping to get out of these six sessions on evangelism?*

MAIN IDEA

The Bible calls all Christians to share the good news about Jesus's death and resurrection with those who don't believe in Christ.

DIGGING IN

At the outset of this study on evangelism, we should begin by defining what "evangelism" is and isn't.

What Is Evangelism? Evangelism is telling others the good news about what Jesus Christ has done to save sinners and calling them to repent of their sins and believe in Jesus.

In order to do this you must tell others that:

- God is holy (1 John. 1:5). He is the creator of all things (Gen. 1:1).
- All people are sinners who deserve God's righteous, eternal wrath (Mark 9:48; Rom. 3:10–19; Rev. 14:11).
- Jesus Christ, who is fully God and fully man, lived a sinless life, died on the cross to bear God's wrath in the place of all who would believe in him, and rose from the grave in order to give his people eternal life (John 1:1; Rom. 3:21–26; 1 Cor. 15:20–22; 2 Cor. 5:21; 1 Tim. 2:5; Heb. 7:26).
- The only way to be saved from eternal punishment and be reconciled to God is to repent of sin and trust in Jesus Christ for salvation (Mark 1:15; Acts 20:21).

This is the gospel, the good news about Jesus Christ. Evangelism is simply telling others this basic message and calling them to repent of sin and trust in Christ. On the other hand, evangelism is not:

- **Personal testimony.** Talking about what God has done in your life may encourage Christians and intrigue non-Christians. And there's certainly a place for this *in* evangelism. But simply sharing about what God has done in your life isn't necessarily evangelism. Evangelism is telling others about what Jesus Christ has done to save *every* sinner who will *ever* turn from their sin and trust in Jesus.
- **Social action.** When we care for the poor, defend the defenseless, and work for a more just society we may commend the gospel, but we haven't yet shared it. Evangelism is telling others the gospel. Contrary to the opinion of some, that can't be done without words!
- **Apologetics.** Defending the faith against unbelievers' objections can lead to evangelism, but apologetics is not evangelism. Apologetics is a useful tool, but if we're not careful it can actually distract us from evangelism, which is telling the good news about Jesus Christ.
- **The results of evangelism.** We *can* share the gospel. We *can't* make anyone believe it. Thinking that we haven't evangelized unless people have been converted is a serious error that can cripple Christians with a sense of failure and guilt. But if we recognize that our job is merely to tell others the good news about Christ and call them to repent and believe, we are liberated to simply preach the gospel and pray for God to change hearts.

1. Do you have any questions about what evangelism is?

Now that we've established what evangelism is and isn't, let's consider a few texts that speak to *who* should evangelize. Acts 8:1–4 gives us a window into the early church's evangelism:

¹ And Saul approved of his execution. And there arose on that day a great persecution against the church in Jerusalem, and they were all scattered throughout the regions of Judea and Samaria, except the apostles. ² Devout men buried Stephen and made great lamentation over him. ³ But Saul was ravaging the church, and entering house after house, he dragged off men and women and committed them

to prison. ⁴ Now those who were scattered went about preaching the word.

2. Who was scattered by the persecution in Jerusalem (v. 1)?

3. Who went about preaching the word, that is, the good news about Jesus (v. 4)?

4. What does this tell us about the early Christians' understanding of who should evangelize?

In Matthew 28:18–20, after rising from the dead, Jesus leaves his eleven disciples with a final charge:

> ¹⁸ All authority in heaven and on earth has been given to me. ¹⁹ Go therefore and make disciples of all nations, baptizing them in the name of the Father and of the Son and of the Holy Spirit, ²⁰ teaching them to observe all that I have commanded you. And behold, I am with you always, to the end of the age.

5. What does Jesus command his followers to make (v. 19)? What does that mean?

6. Of whom are we to make disciples (v. 19)?

7. What are all the things that making disciples involves (vv. 19–20)?

8. To whom does this "Great Commission" apply? Who's responsible to carry it out? Explain your answer from the text itself.

9. Why is Jesus's presence with us especially comforting as we go and make disciples of all nations (v. 20)?

10. Have you ever considered before that all Christians are responsible to evangelize? What's your initial response to that?

11. Have you ever heard someone say they were not obligated to evangelize? What kind of reasons do they give? Why would Satan love to get people to think this way?

12. How can you fulfill the Great Commission as part of your daily discipleship to Christ? Give specific examples.

WEEK 2
WHY SHOULD WE
EVANGELIZE?

GETTING STARTED

1. What are some reasons you don't *evangelize?*

2. What do you think it would take to motivate you to evangelize more?

MAIN IDEA

The Bible gives us many different motivations to evangelize, which is something many of us need because we often lack motivation to evangelize.

DIGGING IN

In this study we're going to consider several biblical reasons *why* we should evangelize.

First, as we considered in the previous study, we should evangelize because the Bible commands us to.

In Matthew 28:19–20 Jesus commands his disciples,

> [19] Go . . . and make disciples of all nations, baptizing them in the name of the Father and of the Son and of the Holy Spirit, [20] teaching them to observe all that I have commanded you.

Paul also exhorts the Corinthians to follow his evangelistic example when he writes,

> [32] Give no offense to Jews or to Greeks or to the church of God, [33] just as I try to please everyone in everything I do, not seeking my own advantage, but that of many, that they may be saved. [11:1] Be imitators of me, as I am of Christ. (1 Cor. 10:32–11:1)

As Christians, our inner beings long to obey all of God's commands. But in the case of evangelism, it can sometimes be difficult to muster up motivation out of a sheer sense of obligation. Thankfully, God's Word gives us several other motivations that spur us on to evangelism. Consider what the apostle Paul writes in Romans 9 and 10:

> [1] I am speaking the truth in Christ—I am not lying; my conscience bears me witness in the Holy Spirit—[2] that I have great sorrow and unceasing anguish in my heart. [3] For I could wish that I myself were accursed and cut off from Christ for the sake of my brothers, my kinsmen according to the flesh. (Rom. 9:1–3)

> [1] Brothers, my heart's desire and prayer to God for them [that is, the Israelites] is that they may be saved. (Rom. 10:1)

1. Why does Paul have great sorrow and unceasing anguish in his heart?

2. Based on Romans 10:1 and what we learn from the rest of the New Testament, what does Paul's concern for his fellow Jews motivate him to do? (See also Acts 13:5; 14:1; 17:1–3; 18:4)

3. What motive for evangelism does this text give us?

4. What are some practical ways you can grow in cultivating and expressing love for non-Christians?

In John 15 Jesus says,

> [8] By this my Father is glorified, that you bear much fruit and so prove to be my disciples. [9] As the Father has loved me, so have I loved you. Abide in my love. [10] If you keep my commandments, you will abide in my love, just as I have kept my Father's commandments and abide in his love. [11] These things I have spoken to you, that my joy may be in you, and that your joy may be full. (John 15:8–11)

5. What are the results of our bearing much fruit through obeying Jesus's commands?

6. How does evangelism in particular bring glory to God?

7. How does the thought that our evangelism glorifies God encourage us to persevere in evangelism?

8. In this passage, Jesus explains that the reason he has given us his commands to obey is that our joy may be full (v. 11). How is the promise of obtaining joy in obedience especially encouraging when you consider evangelism?

Through teaching about obeying Jesus's commands in general, this passage gives us at least two more motivations to evangelize:

1. to glorify God; and
2. to have our joy in Christ made full through obeying his commands.

There's one more biblical motivation for evangelism we should consider together. In 1 Peter 3:13–18a, Peter writes,

> [13] Now who is there to harm you if you are zealous for what is good? [14] But even if you should suffer for righteousness' sake, you will be blessed. Have no fear of them, nor be troubled, [15] but in your hearts honor Christ the Lord as holy, always being prepared to make a defense to anyone who asks you for a reason for the hope that is in you; yet do it with gentleness and respect, [16] having a good conscience, so that, when you are slandered, those who revile your good behavior in Christ may be put to shame. [17] For it is better to suffer for doing good, if that should be God's will, than for doing evil. [18] For Christ also suffered once for sins, the righteous for the unrighteous, that he might bring us to God.

9. What are the two main things Peter commands in this passage?

10. What has Christ done for sinners who trust in him (v. 18)? What is the result for those who trust in Christ (v. 18)?

11. How should Christ's suffering for us and God's acceptance of us through Christ motivate us to both share the gospel with others and be willing to suffer for Christ's sake?

12. What are some ways that sharing the gospel with others and suffering for Christ's sake might go hand in hand?

Think about the various biblical motivations we've covered in this study:

- Obedience (Matt. 28:18–20; 1 Cor. 10:32–11:1)
- Love for others (Rom. 9:1–3; 10:1)
- The desire to glorify God (John 15:8)
- Having our joy made complete through obedience (John 15:11)
- Our acceptance by God through Christ (1 Pet. 3:18)

13. Are any of these motivations to evangelize particularly new or striking to you?

14. What are some ways that you can practically stir up yourself and others to evangelize using these biblical motivations?

WEEK 3
HOW SHOULD WE
EVANGELIZE? (PART 1)

GETTING STARTED

In the next few studies, we're going to consider more practically *how* we should evangelize.

1. As a way to begin thinking about how to evangelize, what's some of the best advice you've received about evangelism?

MAIN IDEA

We should evangelize _____ and _____. (We'll fill in the blanks later.)

DIGGING IN

In 2 Corinthians, Paul describes his own evangelistic commitments as an apostle. In chapter 4 he writes,

> [1] Therefore, having this ministry by the mercy of God, we do not lose heart. [2] But we have renounced disgraceful, underhanded ways. We refuse to practice cunning or to tamper with God's word, but by the open statement of the truth we would commend ourselves to everyone's conscience in the sight of God. [3] And even if our gospel is veiled, it is veiled to those who are perishing. [4] In their case the god of this world has blinded the minds of the unbelievers, to keep them from seeing the light of the gospel of the glory of Christ, who is the image of God. [5] For what we proclaim is not ourselves, but Jesus Christ as Lord, with ourselves as your servants for Jesus' sake. [6] For God, who said, "Let light shine out of darkness," has shone in our hearts to give the light of the knowledge of the glory of God in the face of Jesus Christ. (4:1–6)

1. What has Paul renounced (v. 2)?

2. What does Paul refuse to do (v. 2)?

3. What are some examples of disgraceful, underhanded ways or practicing cunning and tampering with God's Word?

4. Why is it tempting to tamper with God's Word when we evangelize?

5. How does Paul positively describe how he speaks the gospel (v. 2)?

6. What is the goal of Paul's open statement of the truth (v. 2)?

In following Paul's example (see 1 Cor. 10:23–11:1), we should evangelize *honestly*. We should proclaim the truth of the gospel *openly*. We should do this, as Paul says, in order to commend ourselves to others' consciences *before God*. However our unbelieving friends might respond to the gospel, we are accountable to God to share the message faithfully. We should evangelize *honestly*. (Fill in the first blank under "Main Idea.")

7. What are some things that tempt you not to share the gospel honestly? How can you work to overcome those temptations?

In 2 Corinthians 5 and 6, Paul further elaborates on his commitments as an evangelist, writing,

> [20] Therefore, we are ambassadors for Christ, God making his appeal through us. We implore you on behalf of Christ, be reconciled to God. [21] For our sake he made him to be sin who knew no sin, so that in him we might become the righteousness of God.
>
> [6:1] Working together with him, then, we appeal to you not to receive the grace of God in vain. [2] For he says,

"In a favorable time I listened to you,
and in a day of salvation I have helped you."

Behold, now is the favorable time; behold, now is the day of salvation." (2 Cor. 5:20–6:2)

8. In verse 20 Paul says that as an ambassador of Christ, God makes his appeal through him. What is that appeal?

9. What does it mean to implore someone? What does this reveal about how Paul evangelized?

10. What does Paul appeal to the Corinthians not to do (6:1)?

11. According 6:2, why is it urgent that the Corinthians be reconciled to God and not accept God's grace in vain?

Based on Paul's example in these verses, we should evangelize *urgently*. Now is the time of salvation. Now is the time when God extends mercy to all who turn from their sin and trust in Christ. That's why Paul implores the Corinthians to be reconciled to God and appeals to them not to receive the grace of God in vain. (Fill in the second blank under "Main Idea.")

12. Would you say that you typically evangelize urgently? Why or why not?

13. What are some examples of:

    a) A *wrong* urgency in evangelism?
    b) A *right* urgency in evangelism?

WEEK 4
HOW SHOULD WE
EVANGELIZE? (PART 2)

GETTING STARTED

1. What kind of a response does the idea of evangelism typically provoke in you?

2. If that response is a negative one, what do you do with it? How do you seek to overcome it?

MAIN IDEA

We should evangelize _____ and _____. (We'll fill in the blanks later.)

DIGGING IN

In Luke 2, a very familiar passage, angels announce the birth of Jesus. Beginning in verse 8:

> [8] And in the same region there were shepherds out in the field, keeping watch over their flock by night. [9] And an angel of the Lord appeared to then, and the glory of the Lord shone around them, and they were filled with great fear. [10] And the angel said to them, "Fear not, for behold, I bring you good news of great joy that will be for all the people. [11] For unto you is born this day in the city of David a Savior, who is Christ the Lord. [12] And this will be a sign for you: you will find a baby wrapped in swaddling cloths and lying in a manger." [13] And suddenly there was with the angel a multitude of the heavenly host praising God and saying,
>
> > [14] "Glory to God in the highest,
> > and on earth peace among those with whom he is
> > pleased!" (2:8–14)

1. Who and what appeared to the shepherds (v. 8)?

2. How did the shepherds respond to these things (v. 9)? Why did they respond this way?

3. What did the angel tell the shepherds to do (v. 10)?

4. What did the angel "bring" to the shepherds (v. 10)?

5. Why was this news good?

6. Why did this good news mean the shepherds didn't have to be afraid?

The angels' announcement of Jesus's birth vividly demonstrates that the gospel, which means "good news," is a joyful message. It addresses guilty, condemned sinners and announces that they can be at peace with God through the Savior whom he has sent. That's why we should proclaim this message *joyfully*. (Fill in the first blank under "Main Idea.")

7. Why is a joyful evangelist (as opposed to a somber or fearful one) both attractive and appropriate?

8. When you evangelize, do you do so joyfully? Why or why not?

9. Give some practical examples of what it means to evangelize joyfully. How can you seek to grow in evangelizing in these ways?

From Luke 2 we've learned that we should evangelize joyfully. As Paul responds to the plight of his fellow Jews in Romans 9:30–10:1, his example presents us with another aspect of how we should evangelize.

> [30] What shall we say, then? That Gentiles who did not pursue righteousness have attained it, that is, a righteousness that is by faith;

[31] but that Israel who pursued a law that would lead to righteousness did not succeed in reaching that law. [32] Why? Because they did not pursue it by faith, but as if it were based on works. They have stumbled over the stumbling stone, [33] as it is written,

> "Behold, I am laying in Zion a stone of stumbling, and a rock of offense;
> and whoever believes in him will not be put to shame."

[10:1] Brothers, my heart's desire and prayer to God for them is that they may be saved.

10. In light of his fellow Jews' plight before God, what does Paul do for them (10:1)?

11. What is the content of Paul's prayer for his fellow Jews (10:1)?

Following Paul's example, we should evangelize *prayerfully*. (Fill in the second blank under "Main Idea.")

12. Why is it important to pray that others would be saved? (See also Acts 11:18; 16:14; 2 Cor. 4:6; Eph. 2:1–6; Phil. 1:29.)

13. How has prayer impacted your evangelism? How God has answered your evangelistic prayers? Give specific examples.

14. What are some specific ways you can grow, and help others grow, in evangelizing prayerfully and praying evangelistically?

15. What are some ways that your local church as a whole can pray (or already does pray!) for evangelism? How can you personally participate in and encourage these prayers?

WEEK 5
HOW SHOULD WE
EVANGELIZE? (PART 3)

GETTING STARTED

1. *What are some of the hardest aspects of evangelism for you?*

2. *What are some of the most rewarding aspects of evangelism for you?*

MAIN IDEA

In our evangelism, we should _____ and _____.
(We'll fill in the blanks later.)

DIGGING IN

In 1 Corinthians 15 Paul succinctly summarizes the gospel message:

> [1] Now I would remind you, brothers, of the gospel I preached to you,
> which you received, in which you stand, [2] and by which you are
> being saved, if you hold fast to the word I preached to you—unless
> you believed in vain.
> [3] For I delivered to you as of first importance what I also received:
> that Christ died for our sins in accordance with the Scriptures, [4] that
> he was buried, that he was raised on the third day in accordance with
> the Scriptures, [5] and that he appeared to Cephas, then to the twelve.
> (1 Cor. 15:1–5)

1. *What are Paul's sources of knowledge about the gospel?*

2. *What documents is Paul referring to when he says that Christ died and was
raised on the third day in accordance with "the Scriptures" (vv. 3–4)?*

3. What does it mean that Christ died and was raised in accordance *with the* Scriptures *(vv. 3–4)?*

4. How would our understanding of the gospel be impoverished if we didn't have the Old Testament?

While Paul is speaking about the Old Testament in this passage, it's clear from the New Testament itself that the New Testament is crucial for our understanding of the gospel. That the whole Bible is foundational for our understanding of the gospel seems obvious. But what might be less obvious is the implication that we should actually *use* the Bible in our evangelism!

Following Paul's example, in our evangelism we should *use the Bible.* (Fill in the first blank under "Main Idea.")

5. What are some reasons you think it's important to use the Bible in evangelism?

6. What are some practical ways you can use the Bible in evangelism?

At Pentecost in Acts 2, when the Holy Spirit descends and the disciples speak in other languages, Peter gets up to explain what's going on, and he proclaims who Jesus is and what he's done, drawing from the Old Testament. Let's consider the last portion of his address:

> [32] "This Jesus God raised up, and of that we all are witnesses. [33] Being therefore exalted at the right hand of God, and having received from the Father the promise of the Holy Spirit, he has poured out this that you yourselves are seeing and hearing. [34] For David did not ascend into the heavens, but he himself says,
>
>> "The Lord said to my Lord,
>> "Sit at my right hand,
>> [35] until I make your enemies your footstool.'"
>
> [36] Let all the house of Israel therefore know for certain that God has made him both Lord and Christ, this Jesus whom you crucified."

[37] Now when they heard this they were cut to the heart, and said to Peter and the rest of the apostles, "Brothers, what shall we do?" [38] And Peter said to them, "Repent and be baptized every one of you in the name of Jesus Christ for the forgiveness of your sins, and you will receive the gift of the Holy Spirit. [39] For the promise is for you and for your children and for all who are far off, everyone whom the Lord our God calls to himself." [40] And with many other words he bore witness and continued to exhort them, saying, "Save yourselves from this crooked generation." [41] So those who received his word were baptized, and there were added that day about three thousand souls. (Acts 2:32–41)

7. *What does Peter tell the house of Israel to "know for certain" (v. 36)?*

8. *What had the people done to Jesus (v. 36)?*

9. *How do the people respond to the conclusion of Peter's sermon (vv. 37, 41)?*

10. *Keeping in mind that different conversations will require different approaches, what do you think we can learn from Peter's direct address to his hearers? How would you summarize in your own words how Peter directly engaged his hearers?*

One way to describe Peter's approach to his hearers is that he *provoked self-reflection*. He directly confronted them about their guilt. They were cut to the heart, and Peter urged them to repent of their sin and trust in Christ. He provoked them to consider what they'd done, what the consequences were, and what they needed to do in order to be reconciled to God.

Following Peter's example, in our evangelism we should *provoke self-reflection*. (Fill in the second blank under "Main Idea.")

11. *What is it about the nature of the good news that makes it appropriate, even necessary, to provide people with an opportunity for self-reflection?*

12. *What are some practical ways to provoke self-reflection in those with whom we're sharing the gospel?*

13. What would it look like to provoke self-reflection in:

- Someone who seems content to live a pleasure-seeking lifestyle with no thought for God?
- A convinced, scientifically minded atheist?
- Someone who is warming up to the gospel but isn't sure whether they can commit to it?

Can you think of other kinds of people you've evangelized, or would like to evangelize?

WEEK 6
WHAT DOES THE CHURCH HAVE TO DO WITH EVANGELISM?

GETTING STARTED

1. Have you ever brought a non-Christian friend to church?

- How did it go?
- What were his or her impressions of the church?

2. As you interact with non-Christians in your life, what are some of their impressions of:

- Churches in general?
- Your local church in particular?

MAIN IDEA

Jesus calls the church to a corporate life of unity and love in order to display and commend the gospel to the world.

DIGGING IN

In John 13, immediately after Jesus tells the disciples that one of them would betray him, he gives them a "new commandment":

> [31] When he had gone out, Jesus said, "Now is the Son of Man glorified, and God is glorified in him. [32] If God is glorified in him, God will also glorify him in himself, and glorify him at once. [33] Little children, yet a little while I am with you. You will seek me, and just as I said to the Jews, so now I also say to you, 'Where I am going you cannot come.' [34] A new commandment I give to you, that you love one another: just as I have loved you, you also are to love one another.

³⁵ By this all people will know that you are my disciples, if you have love for one another." (John 13:31–35)

1. *What does Jesus mean when he says that God will glorify himself in Jesus, and that where he is going the disciples cannot come (vv. 31–33)?*

2. *What is the new commandment Jesus gives to his disciples (v. 34)?*

3. *In what manner are the disciples to love one another (v. 34)?*

4. *What does it mean to love one another as Jesus has loved us? And how does Jesus's love for us motivate us to love one another?*

5. *What does Jesus say will be the result if we love one another (v. 35)?*

In John 17, Jesus says something very similar to what we've just considered. This time, he says it in a prayer for those who will later become his disciples:

²⁰ I do not ask for these only, but also for those who will believe in me through their word, ²¹ that they may all be one, just as you, Father, are in me, and I in you, that they also may be in us, so that the world may believe that you have sent me. ²² The glory that you have given me I have given to them, that they may be one even as we are one, ²³ I in them and you in me, that they may become perfectly one, so that the world may know that you sent me and loved them even as you loved me. (John 17:20–23)

6. *What does Jesus ask for those who will believe in him through the disciples' word (v. 21)?*

7. *For what purpose does Jesus ask that the disciples would be one (vv. 21, 23)?*

8. *What has Jesus given to his disciples in order to make them one (v. 22)?*

9. Summarize in your own words what these two passages that we've studied teach us about how the corporate life of the church impacts evangelism.

As we've seen, the basic idea in both of these texts is that our love for fellow Christians and unity with fellow Christians serves as a testimony to the world about who Jesus is and what he's done.

It's important to realize that it is in the local church that this unity and love is most concretely lived out. When Christians commit to follow Christ together, and to hold each other accountable to walk in a manner worthy of the gospel—which is what church membership *is*—then this love and unity Jesus commands takes on a very specific and very visible shape.

It's easy to say that you love others and to feel unified with others, until you have to love a specific group of not-yet-perfected Christians! It's easy to talk about love until a specific person you've committed to love in your local church gives you some reasons *not* to love them.

But as we've seen in these passages, our love for fellow church members commends the gospel to the world. With that in mind, let's think more practically about how we can help our local church display the gospel better through our love and unity.

10. How will it hinder our evangelism if our church is full of people who live just like non-Christians?

11. What does the commitment of church membership (both joining and staying through thick and thin) teach the world about the nature of Jesus's love?

12. If a church's internal life of unity and love should commend the gospel to non-Christians, what should a church:

a) Expect of its members?
b) Pray about when gathered together?
c) Talk about in small groups and discipling relationships?

13. Suppose there are four families living on a neighborhood street, two families who belong to the same church and two non-Christian families. How should the relationship between the two Christian families look different than the relationship between the two non-Christian families through the course of the week?

14. In view of the church's calling to be a corporate display of the gospel, what are some ways that you personally can use the church in evangelism?

15. Can you share specific examples of how the church's corporate witness has given you opportunities to evangelize or has aided your evangelism?

TEACHER'S NOTES FOR WEEK 1

DIGGING IN

1. Open this up for any discussion that arises.

2. All the believers except the apostles were scattered by the persecution (v. 1).

3. *All* the believers who were scattered by the persecution went about preaching the word (v. 4).

4. This demonstrates that the early Christians understood that every Christian was responsible to evangelize.

5. Jesus commands his followers to make disciples, that is, people who believe in, obey, and follow him (v. 19).

6. We are to make disciples of all nations (v. 19).

7. Making disciples involves going to all nations, preaching the gospel to them (which is necessary in order for them to *become* disciples), baptizing them, and teaching them to observe everything Jesus commanded (vv. 19–20).

8. This "Great Commission" applies to all Christians. How do we know? Jesus commands his disciples to teach the new disciples to observe all that Jesus commanded, which certainly includes this final instruction. So the eleven disciples are to teach all the new disciples they make to make other disciples.

9. Jesus's presence with us as we evangelize the nations is comforting because:

- Evangelism can be scary
- Some people will reject us and our message
- Evangelizing the nations requires sacrifice and suffering on our part
- And so on . . .

In all this, it's immensely comforting that Jesus is with us. He sustains and supports us. He comforts and encourages us. He reminds us that we are accepted by God through him even though the world rejects us. And he is present in power to save people through the gospel we preach.

10–12. Answers will vary.

TEACHER'S NOTES FOR WEEK 2

DIGGING IN

1. Paul has great sorrow and unceasing anguish in his heart because his fellow Jews don't believe in Christ and are thus faced with God's condemnation.

2. In Romans 10:1 and the texts in Acts, we see that Paul's concern for his fellow Jews motivated him to pray for their salvation and diligently evangelize them.

3. This text shows us that love for the lost, especially concern for their eternal destiny, should motivate us to evangelize.

4. Answers will vary.

5. The results of our bearing much fruit through obeying Jesus's commands are:

- The Father is glorified (v. 8).
- We prove to be Jesus's disciples (v. 8).
- We will have our joy made full (v. 11).

6. Answers will vary, but the basic idea is that evangelism brings glory to God because in evangelism we tell the truth about who God is and what he's done in Christ, and we call others to respond rightly to that truth.

7. Answers will vary. One good reason this should encourage us is that we can know that what we're doing is pleasing to God regardless of how those we're evangelizing respond.

8. Answers will vary.

9. The two main things Peter commands in this passage are:

- Be prepared to give a defense for the hope that is in you (v. 15).
- Be willing to suffer for Christ's sake (vv. 17–18).

10. For sinners who trust in him, Christ suffered death on the cross as a substitute for their sins (v. 18). The result for them is that they are brought to God, that is, reconciled to God and accepted by God (v. 18).

11. Christ's suffering for us should motivate us to both evangelize and suffer for his sake because when we recognize the magnitude of Christ's sacrifice on our behalf, our hearts will overflow with joy, love, and gratitude in the gospel.

12–14. Answers will vary.

TEACHER'S NOTES FOR WEEK 3

MAIN IDEA

We should evangelize *honestly* and *urgently*. (As these ideas emerge through your discussion of the passage, point them out as the two parts of the main idea for this study.)

DIGGING IN

1. Paul has renounced disgraceful and underhanded ways (v. 2).

2. Paul refuses to practice cunning or tamper with God's Word (v. 2).

3. Answers will vary, but examples include:

   - Muting the "bad news" about our sin and God's judgment against it
   - Making the gospel into a message about health and prosperity in this life
   - Presenting Jesus as merely a friend who helps us, rather than the Lord who rules us
   - And so on . . .

4. It's tempting to tamper with the gospel when we evangelize because:

   - The gospel is offensive to non-Christians.
   - We crave other people's acceptance.
   - We want people to come to faith in Christ and we're tempted to try to *make* that happen by making the gospel more appealing to them.
   - And so on . . .

5. As a positive description of how he speaks the gospel, Paul says that he states the truth openly (v. 2).

6. The goal of Paul's open statement of the truth is to commend himself to others' consciences in the sight of God (v. 2).

7. Answers will vary.

8. The appeal God makes through Paul is: "We implore you on behalf of Christ, be reconciled to God" (v. 20).

9. To implore means "to beg urgently or piteously." This shows us that Paul's evangelism was direct, pleading, and urgent.

10. In 6:1, Paul appeals to the Corinthians not to receive the grace of God in vain.

11. The reason it is urgent that the Corinthians be reconciled to God is that *now* is the time when God is extending salvation (6:2).

12–13. Answers will vary.

TEACHER'S NOTES FOR WEEK 4

MAIN IDEA

We should evangelize *joyfully* and *prayerfully*. (As those ideas emerge through your discussion of the passage, point them out as the two parts of the main idea for this study.)

DIGGING IN

1. An angel appeared to the shepherds, and the glory of the Lord shone all around them (v. 9).

2. The shepherds were afraid (v. 9). Throughout the Bible, we see that people are afraid whenever they see an angel or a manifestation of God's glory, because both angels and visible presentations of God's glory bring us face to face with God's holiness. Angels, as messengers of God, usually brought messages of judgment, or even judgment itself, in the Old Testament. And when a sinful person is visibly confronted with a manifestation of God's presence, the reaction we see throughout Scripture is fear, because when we become aware of God's holiness, we are reminded of our sin and the judgment we deserve from God.

3. The angel told the shepherds not to be afraid (v. 10).

4. The angel brought the shepherds "good news of great joy that will be for all the people" (v. 10). The good news is that the long-awaited Messiah, God's anointed king in the line of David, has come, and that he will save his people (v. 11).

5. This news was good because it spoke of a Savior whom God had sent into the world to rescue people from their sins and restore them to peace with God (vv. 11, 13).

6. This news meant the shepherds did not have to be afraid because in Jesus, God came into the world to reconcile men to himself. With the birth of this Savior, God was announcing to them that, despite their sin, they can be reconciled to him through this Savior.

7. A joyful witness is attractive because people are drawn to that which is joyful. It's appropriate because the news we have to announce is good and joy giving.

8. Answers will vary.

9. Answers will vary.

10. In light of the Jews' plight before God, Paul prays for them (10:1).

11. Paul prays that the Jews would be saved (10:1).

12. It's important to pray for others to be saved because *only God can save them.* The Bible teaches that God is the one who grants repentance and faith (Acts 11:18; Phil. 1:29). God opens people's hearts to accept the gospel (Acts 16:14). God is the one who shines the light of the gospel into our hearts (2 Cor. 4:6). And God is the one who brings the spiritually dead to life (Eph. 2:1–6).

13–15. Answers will vary.

TEACHER'S NOTES FOR WEEK 5

MAIN IDEA

In our evangelism, we should *use the Bible* and provoke *self-reflection*. (As these ideas emerge through your discussion of the passage, point them out as the two parts of the main idea for this study.)

DIGGING IN

1. Paul "received" the gospel (v. 3) from Christ himself (see Gal. 1:11–12). His knowledge of the gospel was also confirmed by the Scriptures which predicted the suffering and resurrection of Christ (1 Cor. 15:3–4).

2. Paul is referring to what we call the Old Testament.

3. This means that in a variety of ways, the Old Testament predicts and foreshadows Jesus's sin-bearing death and resurrection.

4. If we didn't have the Old Testament, we wouldn't know as much about:

- God's creation of the world
- Humanity's fall into sin and its consequences
- God's character, which is revealed in his mercy, patience, grace, forgiveness, judgment, and more in the Old Testament record of his relationship with Israel and the nations
- God's promise to send a King (the Messiah) to redeem his people
- God's demand for a sacrifice that atones for sin
- And more . . .

All of these things form the background for, and help us to understand, the good news about Jesus.

5. Answers will vary.

6. There are countless ways to use the Bible in evangelism. Here are just a few:

- Go through one of the Gospels with a non-Christian friend. Ask what he or she thinks about who Jesus is, what he taught, and what his death and resurrection mean.
- Share a passage of Scripture that has impacted you, and use it as a springboard to get to the gospel.

45

- Memorize a simple gospel outline that is based on a few key passages of Scripture.
- When non-Christians ask questions about the gospel or about Christianity, take them to specific passages of Scripture so that they can see the answers for themselves in God's Word.

7. Peter tells all the house of Israel to know for certain that Jesus, whom they crucified, is both Lord and Christ (v. 36).

8. The people had crucified Jesus! (See Matt. 27:24–26.)

9. The people were "cut to the heart" by the end of Peter's sermon (v. 37). And many of them accepted Peter's message, repented of their sin, trusted in Christ, and were baptized (v. 41).

10. Peter engaged his hearers by explaining the meaning of the events they had seen, by charging them with guilt before God because of their sin, and by commanding them to repent and believe in Jesus in order to be saved. What can we learn from this? First, we should tell people what they must do to be saved, and we should urge them to turn from their sin and trust in Christ. Second, we should confront people about their sin. Obviously, this requires tact and sensitivity. But we should not shrink back from telling people that they are sinners before God and that his judgment is against them because of it.

11. The good news makes a claim on each of our lives—*personally*. It makes a claim about who each one of us is as created by God; a claim about how we have personally offended him; and a claim about who we must trust to be reconciled to God. The news of the gospel is both very public and very personal. People need to consider its direct call upon their own lives.

12–13. Answers will vary.

TEACHER'S NOTES FOR WEEK 6

DIGGING IN

1. When Jesus says that God will glorify himself in him, and that where he is going the disciples cannot come (vv. 31–33), Jesus is referring to his impending death on the cross, resurrection, and ascension to the Father.

2. The new commandment Jesus gives to his disciples is that they love one another (v. 34).

3. The disciples are to love one another just as Jesus has loved them (v. 34).

4. To love one another just as Jesus loved us means that we willingly sacrifice ourselves for each other, serving each other and putting others before ourselves.

Jesus's love for us motivates us to love each other because if Jesus, our Master and Lord, was willing to humble himself and die on the cross for our sakes, then we who have been so loved by him are naturally compelled to love our brothers and sisters in Christ in this same way.

5. Jesus says that if we love one another, all people will know that we are his disciples (v. 35). In other words, our love for one another will show the world who we are, and in so doing will show the world something of who Jesus is.

6. Jesus asks that those who will believe in him through the disciples' word would be one, just as he is one with the Father (v. 21).

7. Jesus asks that the disciples would be one in order that the world may believe that God has sent him, and in order that the world may know that God has loved them even as he loved Jesus (vv. 21, 23).

8. Jesus has given his disciples the glory that God have him in order to make them one (v. 22).

9. Answers will vary, but the basic idea is that the way believers live together in the church—their love for one another and unity with each other—broadcasts a message about Jesus to the world. Thus, the life of the church is meant to be a picture, a sign, of who Jesus is, what he came to do, and how he changes people.

10. Answers will vary, but the basic idea is that is that if the church is full of people who live just like non-Christians, or if the church is torn by division and strife, then the church will actually broadcast a false message about Jesus to the world.

11. Answers will vary, but the general idea is that Christ's love is love that *commits* to loving a particular people, that bears patiently with these sinners, and that points them tenderly toward holiness and God's law.

12. If a church's internal life of unity and love should commend the gospel to non-Christians, a church should:

   a) Expect its members to actively engage one another in genuine relationships and sacrificially serve one another as they have needs.
   b) Pray about ways that the church can display the glory of the gospel, such as cultivating unity in diversity, whether that diversity involves age, ethnicity, economics, or other factors.
   c) Encourage people to speak openly about their lives in small groups and other settings. Since our love for one another is a picture of the gospel, we should open ourselves up to the love and encouragement of others by giving them a transparent window into our struggles, circumstances, gifts, and more.

13. Answers will vary, but the general idea is that the two Christian families will, as occasion permits, generally show a greater interest in getting to know one another and serving one another. Together, they have the opportunity to present a picture of Jesus's kingdom life of love and justice in their neighborhoods. For example, they would never sue one another over icy sidewalks (see 1 Corinthians 6) in a way that non-Christians might. They will show generosity in caring for one another's needs. And they may encourage one another toward reaching out to non-Christian neighbors.

In discussing these kinds of specifics, the teacher must emphasize that we are dealing in the realm of Christian freedom where different circumstances may allow for or hinder different kinds of relationships. Also, the teacher should emphasize the fact that God's common grace is universal, applying even to non-Christians (see Matt. 5:45), such that we can praise God when non-Christian families demonstrate love and care which, sometimes, outshines Christians.

14–15. Answers will vary

PERSONAL NOTES

PERSONAL NOTES

PERSONAL NOTES

PERSONAL NOTES

PERSONAL NOTES

PERSONAL NOTES

PERSONAL NOTES

PERSONAL NOTES

PERSONAL NOTES

PERSONAL NOTES